essential careers™

CAREERS AS A
BOOKKEEPER
AND AUDITOR

SUSAN MEYER

ROSEN
PUBLISHING®

NEW YORK

Published in 2014 by The Rosen Publishing Group, Inc.
29 East 21st Street, New York, NY 10010

First Edition

Library of Congress Cataloging-in-Publication Data

Meyer, Susan, 1986–
Careers as a bookkeeper and auditor/Susan Meyer.
    pages cm.—(Essential careers)
Includes bibliographical references and index.
ISBN 978-1-4777-1792-9 (library binding)
1. Bookkeeping. 2. Accounting. 3. Career development—Vocational guidance.
I. Title.
HF5636.M494 2013
657'.2023—dc23

                                                           2013013171

Manufactured in Malaysia

CPSIA Compliance Information: Batch #W14YA: For further information, contact Rosen Publishing, New York, New York, at 1-800-237-9932.

contents

INTRO

Becoming a good bookkeeper or auditor starts with some basic math and strong organizational skills. Could this career be a good fit for you?

DUCTION

E ugene Morse was an internal auditor at the telecommunications company WorldCom, Inc. He was in charge of making sure that all of WorldCom's accounting of its revenues, expenses, profits, and losses was accurate and in order. One morning when he reported to work, Morse discovered evidence of $500 million in expenses that had gone undocumented and unreported.

Going on a hunch, Morse and his manager worked into the late hours for many nights to uncover the mystery of these huge unreported expenses. They sought to discover what was going on without alerting their WorldCom bosses—who they suspected might be responsible. These men ended up uncovering the biggest business scandal of the early 2000s and the largest case of corporate fraud in history. WorldCom had committed fraud by mishandling over $7 billion in funds. Thanks to some honest and careful accounting work, Morse helped put a stop to it.

To prevent fraud, as well as just to keep track of all money streaming into and out of the coffers, all businesses are required to keep meticulous and truthful records of their financial transactions over given periods of time. This process of keeping records is called bookkeeping, and the person that manages the task is called a bookkeeper. Another important role in the managing of a company's financial records is that of the auditor. These trained professionals audit, or perform an official examination, of a company's financial records. Auditors may work for the company that they are auditing or for an outside organization. They have a duty to report any evidence of mismanagement, fraud, or accounting errors that they find.

Jobs in auditing and bookkeeping are incredibly important in all businesses. For this reason, they are also a smart career choice in an uncertain economy. Bookkeepers and auditors can help companies save money. A bookkeeper is in charge of managing the records of a company's business transactions and keeping all paperwork in order. An auditor is in charge of going over a company's financial records and, among other things, making sure the right amount of taxes are paid to the government. Good bookkeepers and auditors help a company uncover fraud or theft. They help a company see where it could save money or where money is being wasted. They can also keep a company from getting in trouble for financial irregularities.

So valued are the men and women who perform these tasks that a report from the Bureau of Labor Statistics, a unit of the Department of Labor, predicts that employment in bookkeeping and auditing will see a 14 percent growth rate between 2010 and 2020. This is partly because financial regulations are becoming stricter. There will be a greater demand for bookkeepers and auditors to help companies satisfy the new rules and manage their accounting services.

Bookkeepers and auditors work for many different industries and businesses. For example, they can work for accounting firms or businesses that help prepare the tax filings of individuals or businesses. They can also work for federal, state, and local governments. They can work for small businesses, where they might handle all the company's day-to-day finances. And they can work for large businesses, where they might be part of a sizable team of other bookkeepers and auditors, with each performing a specialized task.

If you enjoy math and numerical problem solving, have excellent people skills, and are highly organized, you might just have what it takes to be a bookkeeper or auditor. In addition to being a stable career choice, the many different tasks and work environments that a trained bookkeeper and auditor might experience can make for some exciting job options. In this book, you will learn what skills and education a person needs to pursue a career in bookkeeping and auditing, what the job will really be like, and some of the cool career opportunities in the field.

chapter 1

BOOKKEEPING AND AUDITING: A CAREER OVERVIEW

Before setting off on an exciting career in bookkeeping or auditing, it's important to learn exactly what these jobs involve. What is the difference between the two careers? What skills are required? And what might you do on a daily basis? In the introduction, we touched on some of the basics of what a bookkeeper and auditor do. This section will look at these duties in more detail so that you will know if they are something you would like to build a career around.

RECORDKEEPING AND OVERSIGHT

Bookkeepers have been needed for as long as businesses have existed. Before computers, they kept records of financial transactions in actual books or bound ledgers. They had to be very organized to keep all of these books and papers in proper order over years of financial tracking.

Today, instead of actual books, bookkeepers use bookkeeping software and online spreadsheets and databases to keep track of financial records. They track, record, and analyze all financial transactions, from money that a company spends (known as expenditures), bills that the company owes, and money that is owed to the company. They also calculate the

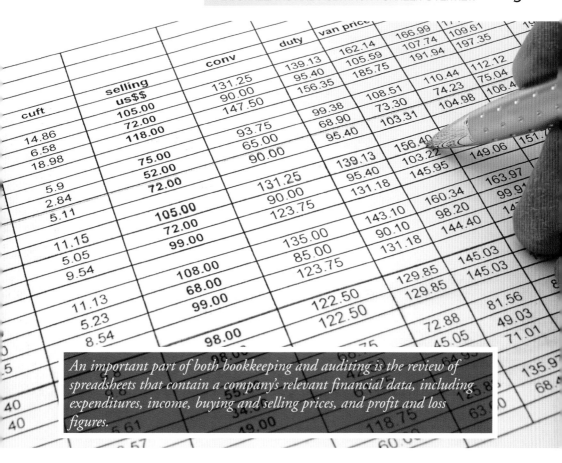

An important part of both bookkeeping and auditing is the review of spreadsheets that contain a company's relevant financial data, including expenditures, income, buying and selling prices, and profit and loss figures.

profit and loss for the company—or how much more or less money the company is taking in than it is paying out. Bookkeepers enter financial transactions into the software and mark them as either debits (costs, or money the company has spent) or credits (income, or money the company has taken in). They then create reports based on this data, known as balance sheets. A balance sheet is a report that compares a company's costs to its income. This helps the company figure out where the money is going and how to lower costs and maximize profits.

Like a bookkeeper, an auditor focuses on a company's financial records and transactions. However, an auditor is usually

Bookkeepers focus on a company's financial records. They gather information from others in the company, review expenses and income, and keep all of the data balanced and well organized.

less involved in the actual recordkeeping and more involved in making sure that all records are accurate. They make notes on anything that doesn't seem correct in the financial files. Having accurate records is very important to a company. Accurate and honest recordkeeping helps a company avoid accusations of fraud and gives it a far clearer sense of how much money is being earned, spent, wasted, or misused.

Not all bookkeepers and auditors will do all of these duties. In small companies or organizations, a bookkeeper or auditor might be in charge of all the accounts. However, in larger companies or in accounting firms, a bookkeeper or auditor might have more specific or specialized tasks. For example, there might be an accounts-payable bookkeeper who deals only with the money a company owes or an accounts-receivable bookkeeper who deals only with the money a company brings in. The responsibilities that auditors or

AUDITORS AND THE 2008 FINANCIAL CRISIS

In the fall of 2008, a global financial crisis rapidly spread throughout the world, beginning in the United States. It led to one of the deepest and longest-lasting recessions in recent history. Much of the crisis was blamed on large banks that failed and/or had to be bailed out when their poor business practices caused billions in losses for their investors. Where were auditors in advance of and during this crisis? Why weren't the problematic business practices discovered sooner?

Auditors have often been blamed for their role in the financial crisis. Some people think they could have done more to identify the banks' reckless risk-taking and unacceptable balance sheets, ring the alarm bells, and restore prudent financial practices before a full-scale and ruinous crisis could develop. An earlier intervention would have prevented many investors from losing money and the world from suffering the worst economic downturn since the Great Depression.

However, it is important to remember that auditors have to work with the data they have been given and make recommendations based on that information. Auditors cannot find every mistake in a company's records, nor can they always see through a company's deliberate deceptions. What they can do is be fearless and persistent in asking tough, probing questions designed to help uncover fraud or mismanagement. An additional challenge that many in the accounting industry are facing today is the increasingly globalized and complicated business environment. Companies often do business around the world and have international subsidiaries, operations, and holdings. Auditors trying to analyze the records of these global businesses need to be familiar with different national economies, accounting standards, taxation policies, reporting techniques, and computer systems in order to do the job properly.

Ultimately what the financial crisis showed is why auditors are so important—in the best-case scenario, they help prevent business failures and broader economic collapse. With more strict, post-recession regulations and a new crop of good, hard-working, and ethical auditors joining the workforce, hopefully more financial errors and reckless decision making will be detected and corrected. This should result in greater financial stability and uninterrupted economic growth.

bookkeepers take on are often related not only to the size of the company for which they work, but also to their level of experience. Entry-level bookkeeper and accounting professionals may initially do a lot of data entry. For example, they might be in charge of entering all the company's bills and transactions into the accounting software. While this isn't the most exciting task, by sticking with the work and gaining more on-the-job skills and experience, a good bookkeeper or auditor can soon move on to more exciting and interesting opportunities.

Some auditors are employed by a company to make sure all of its records are accurate. Their main job is to let the company know if something is wrong so that any problems can be addressed within the company. These auditors are called internal auditors. Some auditors are hired to investigate a company they don't work for. These auditors come in and investigate the company's cash and finances over a certain length of time. These men and women are called external auditors. It is the auditor's job to make sure that the company he or she is auditing is recording and reporting its figures correctly and not doing anything illegal or unethical. If the auditors find something wrong and don't give a company their stamp of approval, that company can get in trouble with the law and with its investors.

WHERE DO BOOKKEEPERS AND AUDITORS WORK?

One of the exciting things about becoming a bookkeeper or auditor is the wide variety of potential work environments. Bookkeeping and auditing jobs can be found almost anyplace where money is being made and spent. Bookkeepers and auditors can be found working for the government, for companies large and small, and even on a freelance basis in which they serve as their own boss. Where you choose to work will have an impact on how much you make, what your hours are, and what your range of tasks will be.

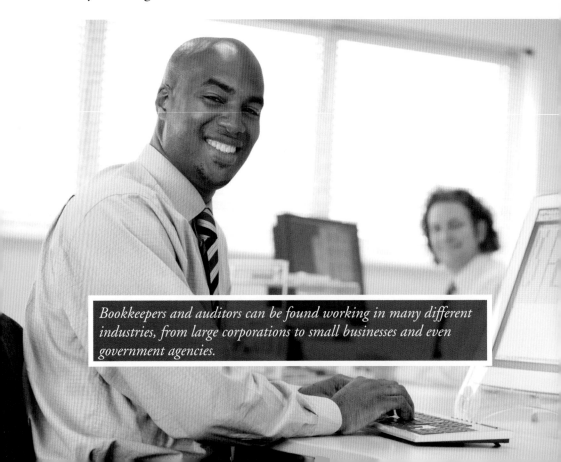

Bookkeepers and auditors can be found working in many different industries, from large corporations to small businesses and even government agencies.

Bookkeepers and auditors may have to work longer hours to meet deadlines at certain times of the year. Many companies work on annual or quarterly (three-month) schedules and need to release financial reports at the end of these periods. Bookkeepers and auditors who work in hotels, restaurants, or stores may find they work longer hours during holidays or busy vacation seasons. This is because there are more financial transactions—more buying and selling of goods and services—and larger payrolls (because of increased hiring) during these peak times.

Some auditors and bookkeepers are employed by firms made up entirely of other auditors, bookkeepers, and accountants. "Accountant" is a more general term for anyone keeping track of financial records. These large firms work with a number of different businesses as their clients. They are independent of the company that hires them to analyze, review, and sign off on its recordkeeping.

There are advantages to working for an auditing or accounting firm rather than working as an in-house auditor, accountant, or bookkeeper for a business. Those who work for auditing or accounting firms get sent to a variety of businesses—from huge, for-profit, multinational corporations to tiny, scrappy, idealistic nonprofit organizations committed to a social cause. So the work itself and the office environment change from week to week or month to month. Sometimes independent auditors and accountants even get to travel to interesting and far-flung places while on the job, meeting with clients nationwide and around the globe.

chapter 2

PREPARING FOR A CAREER IN BOOKKEEPING AND AUDITING

The last section hopefully helped you decide if the world of accounting is for you and if a career as a bookkeeper or auditor is a good fit with your interests, talents, and goals. This section will consider the ways you can make sure that you have the training and skills necessary to make yourself competitive for one of these positions.

THE NECESSARY SKILLS

What basic skills are needed to make it in this exciting but challenging career? With the right background and training, anyone can become a bookkeeper or auditor, but there are definitely some skills that make the journey to the job far easier. For example, it helps to have good math and analytical skills. Analytical skills involve the ability to interpret data correctly and make appropriate and accurate conclusions based on the evidence of that data. When creating reports, bookkeepers and auditors have to be able to look at large amounts of data, identify certain patterns or trends, and determine why money is going to or being taken from certain places. Some companies want their bookkeeper or auditor to also act as a consultant and

You don't have to be a math whiz to aspire to be an accountant, but it helps if you have strong analytical and organizational skills and enjoy working with numbers.

It's hard not to picture a bookkeeper or auditor crunching numbers all day, but that's only a small fraction of what these busy professionals do. In the course of their work, they can even be international travelers and crime fighters!

NOT JUST A BEAN COUNTER

Bookkeepers, auditors, and others in the accounting profession sometimes get a bad rap for having a boring job and crunching numbers all day. Nothing could be farther from the truth! There are many exciting careers in the numbers field that offer fun perks and opportunities. For starters, you might picture a bookkeeper or auditor stuck in the same cubicle at work all day. With a little knowledge of international financial reporting, however, you can become an international accountant. These specialists get to travel as they assist individuals and companies around the globe.

If catching fraudulent bad guys is of greater interest to you, consider becoming a forensic accountant. These crime fighters hunt down white-collar criminals on behalf of public law enforcement agencies. Sometimes they are asked to testify in trials about their findings.

If you're more interested in running the show, certified public accountants (CPAs) can get positions as chief financial officers (CFOs) or comptrollers in businesses or even for the government. These men and women hold the purse strings and control how money is spent. As you can imagine, these jobs come with a lot of power and responsibility. So you see, being good with numbers can take you all sorts of places and offer you many exciting career opportunities.

offer advice on how to manage their money better. Analytical skills are a big help when offering financial advice.

Another important skill for an aspiring bookkeeper is the ability to get along well with people and communicate clearly, comprehensibly, and effectively. This includes being able to write and speak clearly to make yourself understood to someone who is not an accountant. No matter where they find themselves working and whether or not they work on a team or solo, bookkeepers and auditors will always have to work in cooperation with others and explain even the most complicated financial matters in a simple way.

In addition to mathematical, analytical, and communication skills, good bookkeepers and auditors must possess great attention to detail. They are in charge of entering and monitoring very important data. If a single number or decimal is out of place, it can mean a huge, costly, and embarrassing

Solving a difficult math problem requires great attention to detail, and a good mathematician always shows his work. These same skills are useful to bookkeepers and accountants.

error for the company. According to an article in the online magazine *AccountingWeb*, a recent study found that 60 percent of accounting errors result from simple bookkeeping mistakes. Even if a company is not intentionally trying to commit fraud, making an error in, say, the recording of a payment from a customer could lead to unpaid sales tax. This, in turn, could lead to the government charging a fee as a penalty or launching a full audit against the company. Bookkeepers and auditors who pay close attention and make as few mistakes as possible are therefore very valuable to their companies.

It is also very important to have good, basic computer skills. Because almost all accounting work is now done on computers, it is imperative to become comfortable using one and getting used to the relevant financial and accounting software.

COURSEWORK

There are many entry-level jobs available for bookkeeping and auditing clerks that require only a high school diploma. These jobs can lead to higher-paying and more exciting jobs for which the applicant might eventually need to get a college degree.

In order to get an entry-level job, however, it is a good idea to set yourself apart from other applicants. Even while in high school, you can take courses that will help prepare you for your career. If your school offers courses in business or accounting, consider taking one. Taking math courses, even beyond the requirements for graduation, is also a good idea. If your school offers courses in computer or information technology skills, those would also be helpful to take. Filling your schedule with electives relevant to your job will show future employers that you are serious about building a career in bookkeeping or auditing.

Today most accounting, bookkeeping, and auditing work is done with special software on computers. Taking a computer course to make sure you are keeping up with technology is a good way to prepare for this career.

If your school does not have courses in accounting or computers, consider community colleges in your area. Look for basic courses that will help familiarize you with spreadsheets and current bookkeeping software. Being able to put these skills and the knowledge of relevant software on your résumé will go a long way toward setting yourself apart from other applicants.

Once you graduate from high school, you can start looking for a job. Because you can get some entry-level jobs in bookkeeping and auditing with just a high school diploma, you can choose to work for a couple of years, save money, and then go to college to get an associate's (two-year) or bachelor's (four-year) degree in accounting. Many four-year colleges as well as community colleges offer coursework specific to careers in bookkeeping, auditing, and the overall accounting field. Getting a degree in business can also be a good fit for a career as a bookkeeper or auditor.

Taking courses or pursuing a degree in accounting can have a number of advantages. The added knowledge will be useful for you on the job. Also, putting that added educational information on your résumé will help you get higher-paying jobs and be more competitive in the job market. Going to a secondary school after high school, whether it is a two-year or four-year school, can be a good way to make professional connections. Your teachers and professors can introduce you to people in the industry. Also, many colleges have job placement centers. They have career counselors and a network of alumni who work in the field who may be willing to talk to you about what they do and help you locate and secure available positions in the field.

chapter 3

JOURNEY TO A JOB

Whether you plan to go to college before pursuing a job or jump right into the labor market after high school, much of what you will need for the job search is the same. You will need a strong business network, an excellent résumé and cover letter, and great interviewing skills. It is never too early to start working on all of these components to make sure you present the strongest version of yourself to potential employers.

Parents, teachers, librarians, and other adults in your life can be great resources during your job search. They can help you build your business network, hone your résumé, and learn about career options.

CREATING A BUSINESS NETWORK

Begin by working on your business network. Your network is the people around you who can help you learn more about the career you are interested in and even help you get a job. You can start to form your network by looking for someone in the auditing, bookkeeping, or accounting world who will be willing to talk about his or her job with you. Ask your parents, teachers, librarians, or school counselor if they might know of anyone who would be willing to speak to you. You can also ask friends, people at your house of worship or community center, and neighbors. You may be surprised to learn how many potential professional connections you already have.

If your school or community sponsors a career fair, you should attend. It is a good place to do some research. Talking to someone in the field will help you decide if this is a job you would like to have. This person can give you specifics on what it is like to work as a bookkeeper and auditor in your area. He or she can also give details on what salaries and benefits you might expect. Additionally, when you start looking for a job, this person can be a good connection. It's never too early to create a network of good business connections who can help you get started.

BUILDING A BETTER RÉSUMÉ

People in your network can give you advice on making your résumé the best it can possibly be. Your résumé is a summary of everything you have accomplished that is relevant to the job you are applying for. Go to your local library, school counselor, or community career center for advice on the proper format for a résumé. You can also find this information by searching online.

Your résumé should include all information that shows that you would be a good fit for the job. If you are just graduating high school, you might not have a long employment history. If you have a part-time job, put it down. When describing the job, emphasize the ways in which it relates to the job for which you are now applying. Even if you haven't worked as a book-keeper or auditor before, you could explain how, at your summer job selling hot dogs at the softball park, you had to make sure your cash register was balanced at the end of the night, down to the last penny. Also, don't forget to mention any volunteer work you may have done if it is relevant.

In addition to mentioning your high school degree, call attention to any courses you took related to math, business, accounting, or computers. Include any business or accounting courses you took at a two-year or four-year college, even if you didn't graduate or complete a whole degree program. Finally,

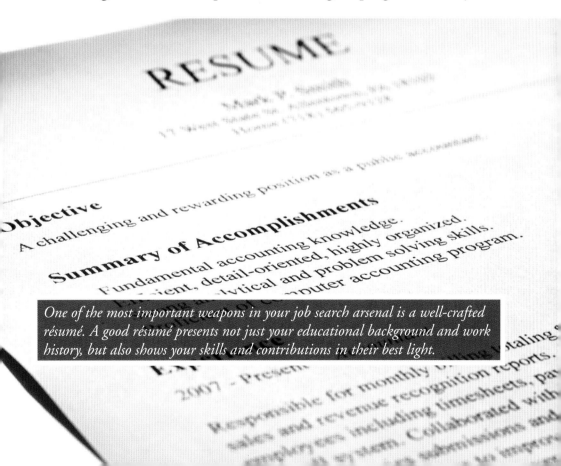

One of the most important weapons in your job search arsenal is a well-crafted résumé. A good résumé presents not just your educational background and work history, but also shows your skills and contributions in their best light.

add any computer programs you know well (such as Microsoft's spreadsheet program Excel and bookkeeping software like Intuit and QuickBooks). Make sure you do not overstate what you know. If you are familiar with a program but don't actually know how to work it, make sure you learn and perfect your skills before putting it on your résumé.

THE COVER LETTER

When applying for a job, you can't just send a résumé; you must also write a cover letter. The cover letter should explain who you are and why you are applying for the job. It should also express interest in the specific position and company. You don't want the cover letter to seem like a generic message you are tacking on to your résumé and sending out everywhere. Do some research and make it unique to each job you apply for and each company you contact. This takes a little more time, but employers appreciate seeing that extra effort.

Make sure to proofread your résumé and cover letter before sending them to a potential employer. Ask friends, family, and people in your network to read them and offer their thoughts. They may catch mistakes and typos that you didn't see. Demonstrating to employers that you have the attention to detail necessary to succeed as a bookkeeper or auditor starts with submitting a flawless résumé and cover letter.

POUNDING THE PAVEMENT

Armed with a stellar résumé, you can begin the job search. Use your business network to help you get some leads. Your family or other connections might just know someone who owns a small business that needs a hardworking bookkeeping clerk.

INTERNSHIPS

An internship is slightly different than a job. While many internships are paid, some don't provide a regular salary. Instead, they provide a small amount of money to live on called a stipend. The real value of an internship is not the pay, however. The real value is the professional experience, on-the-job training, and networking and mentorship opportunities it provides. The people at the company will help teach you some of the things you will need to know on the job. The expectations for an internship are different than for a job. You aren't expected to know everything on your first day; your boss will help guide you.

Finding an internship during the summer or even while you are still in school (if it's something you feel you can balance with your studies) can be a good way to get firsthand knowledge of what it is like to be a bookkeeper or auditor. You can get your feet wet working out financial puzzles and learning the software you will need on-site rather than in classrooms. Some internships even offer college credit.

A good way to find internships is by researching online or by talking to your school counselor or career center. Ask around if anyone in your professional network knows of a firm or company looking for interns. Larger firms are more likely to have established internship programs than smaller companies. However, keep your eyes and ears open for any opportunities that come your way.

You can research jobs online through popular job search Web sites like Monster.com, CareerBuilder.com, and Indeed .com. Many of these sites will allow you to tailor your search for jobs by industry so that you can filter out jobs that aren't

Internships are a good way to learn more about a business. Not only can you decide if the career path is a good fit for you, but you can also be mentored by real auditing and bookkeeping pros.

for bookkeepers and auditors. Look at local businesses that may require the services of a bookkeeper or auditor, as well as accounting firms that employ teams of accounting professionals.

Don't be afraid to cold call even if there are no jobs listed for the company. Cold calling means calling or stopping by a business without already having a connection there. Introducing yourself to potential employers and getting your résumé out there is always a good step. Remember to not be pushy; you want to make a good first impression. Even if the business isn't hiring right now, it might keep your résumé on file and get in touch with you in the future.

ACING THE INTERVIEW

After all the work you put in to applying for a job, when you get a request for an interview, it can feel like you're home free. However, it's important to remember that an interview is not a job offer. It means the company likes what it sees on your résumé and is interested in learning more about you. It is a chance for the employer to meet you in person and see if you are a good fit for the company. It is also an opportunity to see the work environment firsthand and decide if it is a good fit for you. Good interviewing skills can go a long way toward getting an offer.

Make sure to be very prepared for the interview. Research the company and the person interviewing you, if you know who that will be. Consider possible questions the interviewer might ask. You can find lists of common interview questions online. Plan out your answers to these questions. Practice with a family members or friends. Have them ask you some common interview questions so that you can practice saying your answers out loud and responding to another person. The more prepared you are, the less nervous you will feel. The best advice for any interview is to go into it feeling confident in your ability to do the job. If you feel confident in yourself, that will be seen by the interviewer.

Besides being well rehearsed and fully prepared, another way to demonstrate confidence is to dress the part. Generally speaking, the appropriate dress code for an interview is business formal, rather than business casual. Women should wear a pantsuit or jacket and skirt. Men should wear a button-down shirt, dress slacks, jacket, and tie. Your clothing should be clean and pressed. If you are a man, be clean-shaven and groomed. Piercings should be removed and tattoos covered. If you are a woman, keep your makeup professional and not too distracting. Ask advice from a parent or career counselor if you aren't sure if an outfit is interview appropriate.

Make sure to show up on time for the interview or even a few minutes early. Double-check that you know exactly how to get to the interview site the day before so that you will not be

The path from applying for a job to receiving an offer hinges on having good interview skills. It is important to be confident, personable, and professional when meeting an interviewer.

stressed out trying to find it five minutes before the interview is supposed to begin. Also prepare any questions that you might have for the interviewer.

After the interview, be sure to send a follow-up e-mail to everyone you met with, thanking them for taking the time to see you. You should follow up with a thank-you letter even if you have decided that you are not interested in the job or they have decided to hire someone else. Courtesy is important,

and you want everyone you meet with to have a positive impression of you. Somewhere down the road, your paths may cross again, and they may now be in a position to offer you a job. You want them to have good memories of your personality and your professional qualifications and capabilities.

Going out and looking for your first job can be exciting. It can also be frustrating and exhausting. Don't be disappointed if you don't hear back from anyone right away or if someone else is hired instead of you. Rejection is tough. The best way to respond to rejection is by working to improve your résumé, business network, and interviewing skills. That way, you can turn present rejection into future job offers.

chapter 4

GETTING CERTIFIED

Entry-level positions in bookkeeping and auditing often require just a high school degree or college accounting coursework. However, to move into higher positions or make more money, you might choose to get certified.

There are different certifications for bookkeepers and auditors. A bookkeeper becomes certified by meeting a certain number of requirements set forth by the American Institute of Professional Bookkeepers. Those who pass and maintain this certification can call themselves a certified professional bookkeeper, or CPB.

For internal auditors, the certification is done through the Institute of Internal Auditors. This certification lets someone become a certified internal auditor, or CIA. As mentioned previously, not all auditors are internal auditors. Those who are hired to check into company's financial records from the outside are usually a special certified type of accountant called a CPA, or certified public accountant.

Becoming a CPA is a little more complicated than becoming a CPB or CIA. Those interested in certification as a public accountant must apply and take a test within the specific state or region where they would like to work. In addition to working as auditors, people with this accounting certification can work in tax preparation (helping people or businesses calculate, file, and pay their taxes) or even in businesses as a chief financial officer (CFO) or tax manager. This section will look into the different steps that all of these certifications have in common.

Benefits of Certification

Certifications can offer the people who hold them a great deal. First of all, "certified" becomes part of their job title. They can use this title to gain higher-paying positions. Freelance book-keepers and auditors can also charge a higher hourly wage once they become certified.

While the certification is maintained, it indicates to clients and companies that might hire the certified bookkeepers or auditors that they are skilled and current in their knowledge of the field. A certification means these bookkeeping and audit-ing professionals have developed their knowledge and understanding of the best practices in the industry. This raises

Becoming a certified bookkeeper, auditor, or accountant takes a lot of hard work. The AICPA recommends test takers for the CPA exam put in three hundred hours of studying!

them above their noncertified peers and makes them stand out to employers. Certified bookkeepers and auditors are always in demand. In addition to having higher-paying positions, they also find more positions available to them once certification is achieved.

Although there are many benefits to gaining certification, it is a lot of work to undertake. Each certification includes a very difficult exam one must pass. There are also many education and other requirements needed before one can even take the exam. Following the exam, there are further requirements needed to maintain the certification.

Preparing for Certification

To become a certified bookkeeper or auditor, certain classes and programs are required. To become a CPB, an applicant must first take a college course in bookkeeping. This coursework must be accredited. This means the American Institute of Professional Bookkeepers has decided it meets the guidelines for preparing an applicant for certification. You can look online to see if any local colleges offer accredited bookkeeping courses. There are also courses available online.

It is important to make sure the course you are taking is accredited before you take it. If you take a course that is not accredited, you won't be allowed to take the certification exam. Ask a teacher, counselor, or librarian for advice if you aren't sure if a course is accredited or not. Applicants who wish to become certified bookkeepers must also sign a code of ethics. This states that they will perform their job with honesty and integrity.

If you are interested in becoming a CIA, there are more steps required. Candidates for a CIA must have a degree from a four-year college. Again, this college must be accredited, so make absolutely sure your chosen school meets this qualification before enrolling. In addition to the education requirement, a CIA applicant must have two years' work experience in internal auditing. A master's degree in business or accounting can substitute for one of these two years of work experience. Applicants must also submit a character reference form. It must be filled out either by someone who has already achieved certification or by one of the applicant's professors from a college-level business or accounting course. In this form, the recommender must answer questions about the applicant's moral character. Much like the American Institute of Professional Bookkeepers, the Institute of Internal Auditors only wants to certify people who are not only intelligent and capable of doing the job, but also very honest and professional.

To become a CPA, the requirements may vary based on the state or region in which the applicant is applying to work. A good resource for determining the specific requirements for your area is the National Association of State Boards of Accountancy (NASBA). You can access this information on the Internet. If you don't have Internet access at home, visit a public library or school to access the NASBA Web site. Generally, though, the requirements for a CPA are similar to those for a CIA. The applicant typically needs a four-year degree, with a certain number of accounting courses taken during that time. Sometimes additional courses in business law and management are required.

Some certifications require you to take a certain number of accredited courses. Learning under an instructor instead of on the job can give you a more well-rounded view of the industry and every possible task and situation you might run into.

In order to take the main CPA exam, applicants must pass the American Institute of CPAs' exam for professional ethics. The institute is understandably interested in making sure all new CPAs are honest and know how to behave ethically. The applicant usually must submit several letters of recommendation, at least one of which must come from an existing CPA. Applicants must also submit their work history going back as far as ten years. If applicants have not been out of high school for ten years, they can submit a shorter job history. For every job an applicant has held in the accounting industry, he or she must meet certain requirements to prove the quality of his or her work.

As you can see, there is a lot of work involved just to become qualified to take the exam that will make you a certified bookkeeper or auditor. Once you have met these qualifications, there is still a lot of hard work and study ahead. Many of the certification exams are very difficult and require many months of hard work and advance studying. In fact, based on surveys with successful CPA exam candidates, the American Institute of CPAs recommends putting in anywhere from three hundred to four hundred hours studying for the exams.

TAKING THE TEST

Tests for certification are not offered all the time. You will need to do research to find out when and where the test you want to take is offered. The test to become a CPB is a four-part exam. The exam covers everything from basic bookkeeping and error adjusting to fraud prevention.

Two parts must be taken at an official testing center. There are three hundred test centers throughout the country. You can request a free booklet from the American Institute of Professional Bookkeepers that will provide information on the center closest to you. It also offers sample exam questions and test preparation materials. The other two parts of the exam are open-book. They can be done online from your home, school computer lab, or public library. If possible, choose a quiet place free from distractions to take the exam. Applicants must get a 75 percent or higher on the first two parts of the test and a 70 percent or higher on the open-book portions in order to pass the exam.

The CIA exam is offered only twice a year (in May and November). Applicants must register to take it many months in advance. There are over two hundred testing locations for this exam. You can find the nearest testing location by going to the Web site for the Institute of Internal Auditors. This exam is made up of 125 multiple-choice questions on topics

In the months before the exam, you should study hard and take a number of practice tests. Time yourself in each section and look for areas in which you are weak and need to study more.

STUDY UP!

Below are sample questions from CPB, CIA, and CPA tests. As you can see, the tests are not easy. Don't be discouraged if you don't know the answers. There is a reason why people who take this exam not only study for many months but also have already gone through college and often worked for many years in the industry before first attempting the test.

Certified Professional Bookkeeper Exam Sample:

An accounting system that records income when earned and expenditures when the liability is incurred operates on the:

a) Cash basis
b) Cumulative basis
c) Deferred basis
d) Accrual basis

Certified Internal Auditor Exam Sample:

A company's accounts-receivable turnover rate decreased from 7.3 to 4.3 over the last three years. What is the most likely cause for this decrease?

a) An increase in the discount offered for early payment
b) A more liberal credit policy
c) A change in net payment due from 30 to 25 days
d) Increased cash sales

Certified Public Accountant Exam Sample:

A client maintains perpetual inventory records in both quantities and dollars. If the assessed level of control risk is high, an auditor would probably:

a) Insist that the client perform physical counts of inventory items several times during the year
b) Apply gross profit tests to ascertain the reasonableness of the physical counts
c) Increase the extent of tests of controls of the inventory cycle
d) Request the client to schedule the physical inventory count at the end of the year

Answers: D, B, D

related to business and analysis. Applicants must score a 75 percent or higher in order to pass the exam.

For the CPA exam, applicants must apply to the state or region in which they would like to work. After all their materials are approved, they are given a "Notice to Schedule." This means they are allowed to schedule the exam within a certain testing window. They can then take the exam at the official testing center most convenient to their home. The CPA exam is a four-part exam covering auditing, business environment, financial accounting, and tax practices. It usually includes not only multiple-choice questions, but also task-based simulations. These simulations are intended to be similar to what a CPA might encounter on the job. Applicants must get over 75 percent of the exam correct in order to have a passing score.

These are self-study exams. This means you do not have to take a certain course in order to take the exam (beyond those required for certification). Instead, you must prepare on your own. Make sure to give yourself plenty of time to prepare before the exam. You don't want to try to cram all the information in your brain all at once.

There are many courses and exam prep materials available for all the tests. A good resource for finding exam materials is your school or public library. You can also search on the Internet. A good place to start is at the organizations giving the exams. On their official Web sites, they offer links to exam preparation materials and courses. Make sure to research a course or test prep book carefully before spending any money on it. Read reviews and ask around. If you know someone else who has taken and passed the test, ask what he or she would recommend using. It is much better to put the research time in at the beginning than waste valuable study time on poor test prep materials that won't prepare you as well for the exam.

Test preparation courses can help you improve your scores on a certification exam. Make sure to do research first to choose the best one. Taking practice tests in a classroom setting will better simulate the pressure of taking the actual exam.

Prepare as much as you can in advance and try not to cram the day before the test. Get a good night's sleep the night before and have a good breakfast the morning of. Come prepared to the testing site with everything you need (a form of identification, pencils, and anything else you have been asked to bring). Don't be nervous about the exam. The important thing is to give yourself plenty of time to prepare and try your best. Not everyone passes on the first try. You can always study more and take the test again at a later date.

MAINTAINING CERTIFICATION

As soon as you've passed the exam for the certification you're applying for and can prove all other requirements have been met, you can submit your information to the certifying organization. Depending on the certification that you are applying for and where you live, receiving your certification may take anywhere from four to eight weeks.

Once you have the certification, sit back and congratulate yourself. However, while the hardest part of gaining certification is over, you still have to do some work to keep it. For example, if you are a CIA or CPA, you must meet certain continuing professional education requirements. This means all CIAs and CPAs must take a certain number of education hours to prove they are maintaining their knowledge and skills and learning the newest information in the field. This is a little more work for the certificate holder, but ultimately it makes the certification mean more.

Thanks to these maintenance requirements, businesses know that anyone who lists himself or herself as a CIA or CPA on a résumé not only met the requirements at some point in the past but also made sure to stay on top of the frequently changing rules and regulations of the industry.

chapter 5

ON THE JOB

The world of bookkeeping and auditing can be fast-paced, and deadlines are very important. Preparing for the work environment before beginning a new job is a good idea. Of course, as a bookkeeper or auditor, you might be working almost anywhere, so the environment can be varied. However, there are general work and workplace requirements of all employees, regardless of the specific environment or setting in which they work.

DRESS FOR SUCCESS

Most offices have a dress code. This helps prevent distractions in the workplace. Make sure to ask before your first day if there is a dress code and if it is business attire or business casual. You may need to purchase new clothes in order to meet the company's required standard of dress. You will likely be given a desk, cubicle, or office in which to work. While this is your personal space at the office, make sure to not decorate it with any pictures that others might find offensive or inappropriate for a business environment.

BEING A GOOD TEAM PLAYER

Bookkeepers and auditors often work as part of a team. Even if you are the only auditor or bookkeeper in the office, you'll still

Make sure you know the dress code before your first day on the job. Regardless of how formal or casual you are supposed to dress, your clothing should always be clean and neatly pressed.

have people whom you will work with on a daily basis and need to report to. It's important to make a good first impression with your coworkers and maintain a positive working relationship. Be friendly, but remember not to treat coworkers like your normal friends. You shouldn't make jokes around the office that might offend someone. You also can't assume all of your coworkers will share the same political or religious views. These are conversations best kept out of the office.

HOURS AND DUTIES

As a bookkeeper or auditor, you will be expected to keep regular business hours. This might be nine to five or a little later depending on where you work. However, in the bookkeeping and auditing industry, there is usually a normal season and a busy season. Certain businesses will require more work during certain months of the year because of the particular rhythms and requirements of their business operations, the tax year or fiscal year, or financial cycles. During these busy times of the year, you may be asked to put in extra hours to meet important deadlines.

Tasks you can expect to have when you first start can vary due to your position. However, if you are working as an entry-level bookkeeping or auditing clerk, you can reasonably expect certain standard duties. For example, a bookkeeper will be expected to use bookkeeping software and online spreadsheets and databases to record financial

When you first start your job, your tasks may be relatively few and simple. Once you learn about the company and gain new knowledge and experience, the job will often evolve to fit your growing skill set.

transactions. He or she will also receive incoming cash and checks and record them as income. Additionally, the book-keeper will record costs and anything the company spends money on as debits. Credits and debits will be assigned to the appropriate account within the company. A bookkeeper or auditor may produce balance sheets. Finally, he or she may be asked to check figures and reports to make sure that everything is correct. The bookkeeper or auditor will make a note if he or she finds any errors or differences in the records or reports. He or she will then prepare a report outlining these notes.

Bookkeepers and auditors prepare financial records for the paying of government taxes. In some small businesses, they may be in charge of actually preparing tax returns. A book-keeper can help answer the questions of an internal auditor or accountant. Since the bookkeeper is the one who manages records and records the data, he or she is the one best able to

Bookkeepers and auditors don't just crunch numbers alone at their desks all day. Their jobs also involve talking to others to point out errors and to ask questions to figure out irregularities in the financial records. Teamwork and communication are vital to the success of bookkeepers and auditors.

Q&A WITH A CIA

The author talked to an internal auditor working for a large New York firm about his career.

Q: What's an average day like at your job?
A: The day starts by arriving at either my home office or the client's site, depending on the project I'm working on. An auditor will normally have multiple interactions with his or her client contact throughout the day. Daily tasks range from conducting interviews to making sure I fully understand how a process works, performing tests of business transactions or activities to ensure that processes are working as designed, or analyzing a company's financial statements to make sure they are accurate.

Q: What's your favorite thing about your job?
A: The relationships I make, both coworkers and clients, cannot be matched in any other field. I have had a chance to work with and for such a wide array of people, and it has helped shape who I am today. Working in a tight team group forms quick friendships, and being able to really help a client is always a great feeling. Also, the ever-changing projects continually present me with new challenges and learning opportunities.

Q: What are the perks of your job?
A: Accounting provides a great baseline knowledge for all aspects of business. It is a very strong starting-out point for any future jobs in the finance department of a company. Also, there are great opportunities for travel. Over the first half of my career, I probably traveled 30 to 50 percent of my time all across the United States. Over the past few years, accounting has allowed me to visit more than twenty countries while serving global clients.

answer questions for an auditor. A big part of an auditor's job isn't just looking at spreadsheets all day. He or she must ask a lot of questions and follow up on answers in order to get a full and accurate picture of the company's financial records and needs. This is why good communication skills are important for both bookkeepers and auditors.

BENEFITS AND COMPENSATION

A job in the bookkeeping and auditing industry can vary a great deal in terms of how much you will make and what benefits you will receive. The type of company where you work—from a large accounting firm to a small, family-owned business—as well as the state and locality where you are employed, will have an impact on your total salary. A good place to find a general idea of salary is the Bureau of Labor Statistics' *Occupational Outlook Handbook*, accessible online through the BLS's Web site. This site provides information on salary ranges for a particular occupation, as well as projected job growth, work environment, educational requirements, and duties and responsibilities.

chapter 6

THE FUTURE OF BOOKKEEPING AND AUDITING

As you have gathered from previous sections, it takes a lot of work and some time to climb the ladder in the accounting world. Becoming a bookkeeper or auditor doesn't happen overnight. This may lead you to wonder about the future of the industry. Sure, it's a stable and in-demand job today, but what about tomorrow? This section will answer that question and look at the ways in which technology is changing and expanding the role of bookkeepers and auditors.

TECHNOLOGY: FRIEND OR FOE?

New computer programs and bookkeeping and auditing software can calculate and analyze numbers with ease. Does this mean that human bookkeepers and auditors will soon be replaced with computers?

The answer is no. The future for the bookkeeping and auditing industry is anything but uncertain. Companies still require skilled human workers even with all the new technology. In fact, as mentioned in the introduction, the Bureau of Labor Statistics predicts growth for the industry through 2020, with potentially 250,000 new jobs added between now and then. There are currently around two million people working as bookkeepers and auditors. Because this field is so large, it means there will often be a high number of job openings as so many people get promoted out of entry-level jobs or shift to other business- or finance-related positions. This means it is easier to get an entry-level job in bookkeeping and auditing than it is in many other industries.

Job growth for bookkeepers and auditors is tied to the growth of business. If there aren't a lot of businesses and

Bookkeepers don't keep physical books anymore. Instead most book-keeping and auditing work is performed with the help of special computer software, and the records are stored digitally.

organizations making financial transactions, they won't need people to input and analyze this activity. As the number of organizations and businesses increases, so, too, will the number of job opportunities for bookkeepers and auditors. However, even in times of financial crisis, when some companies go out of business and relatively healthy enterprises reduce their buying and selling, there is often a greater need for accounting professionals.

For example, in response to the recent financial crisis that began in 2008, investors wanted more care and attention to be paid to the bookkeeping of the companies in which they invested. This has led to more strict financial reporting regulations placed on companies. This, in turn, translates into more opportunities for auditors to go over the finances of a company and make sure they meet the latest laws and requirements.

BOOKKEEPING AND AUDITING IN THE INTERNET AGE

Some tasks performed by bookkeepers and auditors, especially entry-level clerks, have changed as a result of new technology. Electronic banking and bookkeeping software has done away with the need for actual books in which financial records are kept. Instead, this is all done on computers. Also, most financial transactions are now conducted online, rather than by the sending of physical checks or other forms of payment. However, regardless of how a payment is made or received, bookkeepers, auditors, and accounting clerks are still needed to make sure everything adds up correctly and is recorded properly.

Bookkeepers and auditors are never going to be threatened by new technological advances because a human eye will always be needed to go over everything carefully and ask the right questions to uncover any unintentional errors or intentional

Changing technologies affect every industry, and the accounting profession is no exception. Mobile technology like smartphones and tablets makes it easier for bookkeepers and auditors to manage data while in meetings, traveling, or working at home or remotely.

fraud. In fact, new software makes the job of auditors and bookkeepers far easier. Ultimately, it also makes their tasks more efficient and frees up their time to expand their role and take on new challenges.

For this reason, it's actually a very exciting time to be considering a career in auditing, bookkeeping, and general accounting. Far from just number crunching, accounting and tax professionals may move beyond financial reporting and data gathering. Some can take on a role in offering financial advice to their clients. This would shift them into a different business environment and change their duties from data collection to analysis of business information.

THE ROLE OF SOCIAL MEDIA

Social media and mobile technology will continue to change how bookkeepers and auditors interact with each other and with clients. The widespread popularity and utility of smartphones, tablets, and other mobile devices are changing how businesses and offices are run. Today, business communication happens all the time, not just when a worker or client is in the office. Some companies and organizations even allow workers to BYOD (bring your own device) and use these personal mobile devices for work.

There are issues that result from these policies because the work of bookkeepers and auditors is often classified. Protecting sensitive financial information is a high priority for most businesses and for the auditors and bookkeepers who work for them. According to a survey about top technology initiatives published by the American Institute of CPAs, managing information security on the Internet has become a huge priority as more data is handled over the Internet. There are many advantages to going paperless: saving money, being more environmentally responsible, and

COMPUTING IN THE CLOUD

These days, people talk about the "cloud" on the Internet almost as often as they talk about the weather. But what exactly is it? "Cloud" is Internet slang for the storage of files that can be accessed over the Internet. Most companies store their computerized records on a server. A server is a big computer capable of storing a lot of information. Different people at the company can access the server from their own computers to find the files and records they need. The cloud isn't a computer; it is a virtual server. Instead of storing files in a physical machine, the files are stored on the Internet.

The advantages of cloud storage are many. It is cheaper for a company to maintain a service over the Internet than build and maintain records on a server. It also makes it easier to work with clients all over the world or with freelancers working from home. Unlike a physical server, which can present challenges in being accessed from far away, the cloud can be accessed from anywhere. All you need is a computer with Internet access and a password to log in. Using cloud storage also means constant software updates, so everyone viewing the data knows he or she is using the same and most recent version of a document. This enables bookkeepers and auditors to work more quickly and effectively with clients and businesses near and far.

sending information much faster. However, handling security issues will definitely continue to be an issue to watch. Bookkeepers and auditors must remain knowledgeable and current on the best practices for preserving data security and client privacy.

Social media also affects how job seekers reach out to prospective employers and build a professional network. The blog *SocialCPAs*, a source for helping accounting professionals better understand and use social media, conducts an annual

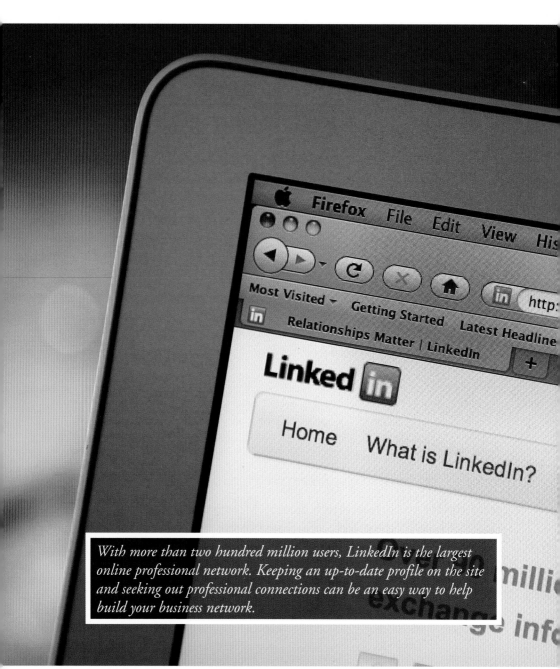

With more than two hundred million users, LinkedIn is the largest online professional network. Keeping an up-to-date profile on the site and seeking out professional connections can be an easy way to help build your business network.

survey on social media use among CPAs. What it has determined is that many accounting professionals use social media sites related to their work. LinkedIn is currently the most popular. This professional networking site was used by more

than 90 percent of survey responders. LinkedIn is a site that allows people to bring their business network online, build a résumé profile, and connect to others in the industry. As you begin your job search, it is a good idea to join this site and build a profile. It would also be wise to continue to monitor social media trends because, with the changing nature of the Internet, the most popular social media site for business networking today might just be an Internet ghost town tomorrow. Staying current with the latest social media and technology trends is the best way to stay competitive in the business world.

Joining the exciting trends and technologies of the new auditing and bookkeeping workplace is a worthwhile pursuit. As businesses and economies grow, so will the need for more reliable, honest, and accurate bookkeepers and auditors. As long as money is being spent, men and women will be needed to keep track of it. As with any career, becoming an auditor or

Becoming a bookkeeper or auditor can be a rewarding career choice. With 14 percent job growth projected over the next decade, it can be both a secure and expanding career field for someone with the right skills and interests.

bookkeeper means a lot of hard work. The path that begins with taking an accounting course in high school and realizing you have a knack for numbers and leads to you becoming a certified internal auditor or public accountant is a long one. However, for the right person—one who enjoys the quiet of analyzing numbers, the excitement of fast-paced deadlines, and the satisfaction and camaraderie of being part of a team—it can be a very rewarding and fulfilling professional journey.

glossary

accredited Officially recognized or authorized.

alumni Graduates of a certain school.

audit To oversee financial records in order to spot and correct errors and ensure the accuracy of financial reporting.

balance sheet A report comparing a company's costs to its income.

certification An official qualification given by a professional organization that indicates the certified person has passed a qualifying exam and possesses certain required knowledge to perform well in a given field.

cloud computing The practice of using an Internet-hosted server to store and manage data.

cold call To make contact with a person or business without a prior invitation or appointment.

consultant Someone who offers professional advice.

credits Income; money that a company has earned.

debits Costs; money that a company has spent.

entry-level Being at the lowest level of a hierarchy; a low-level starting position.

expenditure Money spent.

fraud The act of lying or intentionally holding back or distorting information in order to gain money.

freelance To work on a contract basis with one or more companies; not employed full-time, with salary and benefits, by any one company.

internal auditor A person who performs audits on the company for which he or she works.

internship A position giving on-the-job training and supervised practical experience to someone who is still in school or just setting out in a professional field.

recession A period of economic decline and contraction.

regulations Rules set forth by the government.

simulation An imitation that is meant to mimic a process or the functioning of a system, for testing, practice, or training purposes.

social media Forms of electronic communication through which users create online communities to share information, ideas, personal messages, and other content.

software Computer programs; the entire set of programs, procedures, and related documentation associated with a system, especially a computer system.

stipend An allowance.

white-collar crime Fraud or other business wrongdoing.

for more information

American Accounting Association
5717 Bessie Drive
Sarasota, FL 34233-2399
(941) 921-7747
Web site: http://aaahq.org
The American Accounting Association encourages improved
    education, research, and practice in the accounting indus-
    try. It was founded in 1916 and was originally known as
    the American Association of University Instructors in
    Accounting.

American Institute of Certified Public Accountants (AICPA)
1211 Avenue of the Americas
New York, NY 10036-8775
(212) 596-6200
Web site: http://www.aicpa.org
The AICPA is the largest member organization for the
    accounting profession, with members in 128 countries. It
    sets ethical standards for the profession and offers special
    credentials for CPAs who focus on certain aspects of the
    profession, from personal finance planning to fraud
    management.

American Institute of Professional Bookkeepers (AIPB)
6001 Montrose Road, Suite 500
Rockville, MD 20852
(800) 622-0121
Web site: https://www.aipb.org

The AIPB is an organization recognizing the profession of bookkeeping and providing the certification program for elite professional bookkeepers. It also provides continuing education programs for bookkeepers.

Auditing Association of Canada
129 Timber Drive
London, ON N6K 4A3
Canada
(866) 582-9595
Web site: http://www.auditingcanada.com
The Auditing Association of Canada is a self-regulating member organization in which member auditors work together to improve the industry. It encourages professional development, active volunteer participation, and maintaining a bilingual, Canadian presence.

Bureau of Labor Statistics (BLS)
2 Massachusetts Avenue NE
Washington, DC 20212-0001
(202) 691-520
Web site: http://www.bls.gov
The Bureau of Labor Statistics is a division of the U.S. Department of Labor. It collects and analyzes economic information, including that related to specific professions and their potential for job and salary growth.

Canada Business Network
601 West Cordova Street, Suite 82
Vancouver, BC V6B 1G1
Canada
(888) 576-4444
Web site: http://canadabusiness.ca

The Canada Business Network is an organization devoted to promoting businesses by providing them the resources to grow and prosper. Its site includes labor statistics for job growth and expectations for industries including accounting, bookkeeping, and auditing.

Canadian Bookkeepers Association
482-283 Danforth Avenue
Toronto, ON M4K 1N2
Canada
(866) 451-2204
Web site: http://c-b-a.ca
The Canadian Bookkeepers Association is a nonprofit organization committed to improving the Canadian bookkeeping industry. It seeks to provide information on procedures, education, and technologies to enhance the industry as well as the individual bookkeeper.

Chartered Accountants of Canada
277 Wellington Street West
Toronto, ON M5V 3H2
Canada
(416) 977-3222
Web site: http://www.cica.ca
This organization unites accounting professionals around Canada to help provide licensing standards and consistent standards for professional conduct in the industry. It helps keep all Canadian CPAs on the same page and current on the latest standards in the industry.

Institute of Internal Auditors (IIA)
247 Maitland Avenue
Altamonte Springs, FL 32701-4201

(407) 937-1111

Web site: https://na.theiia.org

The IIA was established in 1941 and has 175,000 members
around the world. The organization provides training, certification, research, and career opportunities to internal auditors.

Institute of Professional Bookkeepers of Canada (IPBC)

P.O. Box 31014

RPO Thunderbird

Langley, BC V1M 0A9

Canada

(866) 616-4722

Web site: http://www.ipbc.ca

The IPBC is a member organization whose mission is to
provide ongoing education and resources to help promote
excellence in bookkeeping. The Canadian nonprofit also
works to raise awareness about the certification opportunities available to professional bookkeepers.

International Federation of Accountants

529 5th Avenue, 6th Floor

New York, NY 10017

(212) 286-9344

Web site: http://www.ifac.org

The International Federation of Accountants is a global
organization aimed at strengthening the accounting profession. The organization is made up of 2.5 million
accountants in 129 countries and working in a number of
different fields.

National Association of Certified Public Bookkeepers

140 North Union Avenue, Suite 240

Farmington, UT 84025

(866) 444-9989

Web site: http://www.nacpb.org

The mission of the National Association of Certified Public Bookkeepers is to ensure that only truly qualified individuals are allowed to provide bookkeeping services. The NACPB also provides professional development resources to public bookkeepers to help them do their job better.

National Association of State Boards of Accountancy (NASBA)

150 Fourth Avenue North, Suite 700

Nashville, TN 37219-2417

(615) 880-4200

Web site: http://www.nasba.org

Founded in 1908, the NASBA oversees the boards of accounting for all the individual states and regions in the United States that oversee the certification of new public accountants.

WEB SITES

Due to the changing nature of Internet links, Rosen Publishing has developed an online list of Web sites related to the subject of this book. This site is updated regularly. Please use this link to access the list:

http://www.rosenlinks.com/EC/Audit

for further reading

Axman, Melanie. *A Short Guide to Editing Your Résumé.* Seattle, WA: Amazon Digital Services, 2012.

Bennington, Emily, and Skip Lineberg. *Effective Immediately: How to Fit In, Stand Out, and Move Up at Your First Real Job.* Emeryville, CA: Ten Speed Press, 2010.

Beshara, Tony. *Unbeatable Résumés: America's Top Recruiters Reveal What Really Gets You Hired.* New York, NY: AMACOM, 2011.

Brezina, Corona. *America's Recession.* New York, NY: Rosen Publishing, 2011.

Byers, Anne. *Great Résumé, Application, and Interview Skills.* New York, NY: Rosen Publishing, 2007.

Costa, Carol. *Alpha Teach Yourself Bookkeeping.* New York, NY: Alpha Books, 2008.

Crumbley, Larry. *Forensic and Investigative Accounting.* Chicago, IL: CCH, 2009.

Dauber, Nick A. *The Complete CPA Reference.* Hoboken, NJ: John Wiley & Sons, 2012.

Doupnik, Timothy, and Hector Perera. *International Accounting.* New York, NY: McGraw-Hill, 2011.

Doyle, Allison. *Internet Your Way to a New Job.* Cupertino, CA: Happy About, 2011.

Ferguson Publishing. *Professional Ethics and Etiquette* (Career Skills Library). New York, NY: Ferguson Publishing, 2009.

Ferrell, O. C., and John Fraedrich. *Business Ethics: Ethical Decision Making and Cases.* Mason, OH: Cengage Learning, 2013.

Flannery, David A. *Bookkeeping Made Simple.* New York, NY: Random House, 2005.

Ganoff, Michael H., and Saleha B. Khumawwala. *Government and Not-for-Profit Accounting: Concepts and Practices.* New York, NY: John Wiley & Sons, 2011.

Glesson-White, Jane. *Double Entry: How the Merchants of Venice Created Modern Finance.* New York, NY: W. W. Norton & Company, 2012.

Greenwood, Mary. *How to Interview Like a Pro: Forty-Three Rules for Getting Your Next Job.* Bloomington, IN: iUniverse, 2010.

Harmon, Daniel E. *Internship and Volunteer Opportunities for Science and Math Wizards.* New York, NY: Rosen Publishing, 2013.

Hill, Paul. *The Panic Free Job Search: Unleash the Power of the Web and Social Networking to Get Hired.* Pompton Plains, NJ: Career Press, 2012.

Jaumann, Sylvia. *Secrets to Starting & Running Your Own Bookkeeping Business: Freelance Bookkeeping at Home.* Kamloops, BC, Canada: First Rate Books, 2010.

Knapp, Michael C. *Contemporary Auditing.* Mason, OH: Cengage Learning, 2011.

Misner, Ivan, et al. *Networking Like a Pro: Turning Contacts into Connections.* Irvine, CA: Entrepreneur Press, 2010.

Mohn, Angie. *Bookkeepers' Bootcamp: Get a Grip on Accounting Basics.* Vancouver, BC, Canada: International Self-Counsel Books, Ltd., 2010.

Orloff, Judith, and Darrell Mullis. *The Accounting Game: Basic Accounting Straight from the Lemonade Stand.* Naperville, IL: Sourcebooks, 2008.

Pickett, K. H. Spencer. *The Essential Guide to Internal Auditing.* West Sussex, England: John Wiley & Sons, 2011.

Pinson, Linda. *Keeping the Books: Basic Recordkeeping and Accounting for the Successful Small Business.* New York, NY: Dearborn Trade Books, 2007.

Piper, Mike. *Accounting Made Simple: Accounting Explained in 100 Pages or Less.* New York, NY: Simple Subjects LLC, 2013.

Rittenberg, Larry E. *Auditing: A Business Risk Approach.* Mason, OH: Cengage Learning, 2011.

Schultze, Quentin J. *Résumé 101: A Student and Recent-Grad Guide to Crafting Résumés and Cover Letters.* New York, NY: Crown Publishing, 2012.

Standard, Ian. *Young Professionals.* Surrey, England: Trotman Publishing, 2010.

Wells, Joseph. *Principles of Fraud Examination.* Hoboken, NJ: Wiley, 2010.

Zack, Devora. *Networking for People Who Hate Networking: A Field Guide for Introverts, the Overwhelmed, and the Underconnected.* San Francisco, CA: Berrett-Koehler, 2010.

bibliography

Addison, Matthew. "What Is a bookkeeper?" The Institute of Certified Bookkeepers, 2013. Retrieved May 2013(http://www.icb.org.au/About%20Us/What%20is%20a%20Bookkeeper).

AICPA. *Auditor's Report: Comprehensive Guidance and Examples.* New York, NY: AICPA, 2012.

AICPA. *Investment Companies Industry Developments: Audit Risk Alert.* New York, NY: AICPA, 2012.

AIPB. *Certified Bookkeeper's Designation.* Rockville, MD: AIPB, 2008.

Berger, Lauren. *All Work, No Pay: Finding an Internship, Building Your Resume, Making Connections, and Gaining Job Experience.* New York, NY: Random House, 2012.

Bureau of Labor Statistics. *Occupational Outlook Handbook.* December 2012. Retrieved March 2013 (http://www.bls.gov/ooh/office-and-administrative-support/bookkeeping-accounting-and-auditing-clerks.htm).

DeFelice, Alexandra. "Social Media: Where Does Your Firm Stand?" *AccountingWeb*, January 7, 2013. Retrieved March 2013 (http://www.accountingweb.com/article/social-media-trends-where-does-your-firm-stand/220655).

Fedorko, Jamie. *The Intern Files: How to Get, Keep, and Make the Most of Your Internship.* New York, NY: Simon Spotlight Entertainment, 2007.

Flannery, David A. *Bookkeeping Made Simple.* New York, NY: Random House, 2005.

Hill, Paul. *The Panic Free Job Search: Unleash the Power of the Web and Social Networking.* Pompton Plains, NJ: Career Press, 2012.

IIA Research Foundation. *Sawyer's Guide for Internal Auditors.* New York, NY: IIA Research Foundation, 2012.

Institute of Internal Auditors. "A World in Economic Crisis: Key Themes for Refocusing Internal Audit Strategy." Altmonte Springs, FL: Global Audit Information Network, 2009.

Ittelson, Thomas R. *Financial Statements: A Step-by-Step Guide to Understanding and Creating Financial Reports.* Franklin Lakes, NJ: Career Press, 2009.

Liana, Eleferie, and Ruse Elena. "Accounting and Audit Versus Global Economic Crisis." Ovidius University Annais Economic Science Series. Constanta, Romania, 2012.

NASBA. "Uniform CPA Exam." Retrieved March 2013 (http://www.nasba.org/education/becomingacpa /whatistheuniformcpaexam).

Pickett, Spencer K. H. *The Essential Guide to Internal Auditing.* Hoboken, NJ: Wiley, 2011.

Pickett, K. H. Spencer. *The Internal Auditor at Work: A Practical Guide to Everyday Challenges.* West Sussex, England: John Wiley & Sons, 2003.

Pinson, Linda. *Keeping the Books: Basic Recordkeeping and Accounting for the Successful Small Business.* Fort Lauderdale, FL: Dearborn Trade Publishing, 2005.

Piper, Mike. *Accounting Made Simple: Accounting Explained in 100 Pages or Less.* New York, NY: Simple Subjects LLC, 2013.

Russell, J. P. *The Internal Auditing Pocket Guide: Preparing, Performing, Reporting, and Follow-up.* Milwaukee, WI: Quality Press, 2007.

Schultze, Quentin J. *Resume 101: A Student and Recent-Grad*

Guide to Crafting Resumes and Cover Letters. New York, NY: Crown Publishing, 2012.

Scott, Peter R. *Auditing Social Media: A Governance and Risk Guide.* Hoboken, NJ: Wiley, 2011.

Social CPAs. "Are You Doing Anything to Monitor Your Name or Reputation on Social Media Sites?" SocialCPAs .com, January 3, 2013. Retrieved March 2013 (http:// www.socialcpas.com/2013/01/monitor-name-reputation .html).

University of Michigan-Flint. "Preparation to Become a Certified Public Accountant." 2010. Retrieved May 2013 (http://www.umflint.edu/som/cpa_exam.htm).

U.S. District Court, Southern District of New York. "WorldCom, Inc., Securities Litigation." September 21, 2005. Retrieved March 2013 (http://www.worldcomlitigation .com/courtdox/2005-09-21CoteOpApprovSetts.pdf).

index

A

accounts-payable bookkeeper, 11
accounts-receivable bookkeeper, 11
American Institute of CPAs, 40, 58
American Institute of Professional
    Bookkeepers, 35, 37, 38, 40
analytical abilities, 16, 20
associate's degree, 23
auditors
    career outlook for, 6, 53–56
    education, 21–24
    skills needed, 7, 16, 20–21
    unique careers, 19
    what they do, 5–6, 9–14
    where they work, 6–7

B

bachelor's degree, 23, 37, 39
balance sheets, 9, 12, 50
benefits, 26, 52
bookkeepers
    career outlook for, 6, 53–56
    education, 21–24
    skills needed, 7, 16, 20–21
    unique careers, 19
    what they do, 5, 6, 8–9, 11,
      13–14
    where they work, 6–7

C

CareerBuilder.com, 29
career fairs, 26
certifications, 35
    advantages to, 36–27
    keeping up, 45
    sample test questions,
      42–43
    studying for, 37–40
    testing for, 40–45
certified professional bookkeeper
    (CPB), 35, 37, 40
certified public accountant
    (CPA), 19, 35–36, 38–40,
      43, 45, 63
character reference form, 38
chief financial officers (CFO),
    19, 35–36
clothing, picking job-appropriate,
    31–32, 46
cloud computing, 59
cold calling, 30
communication skills, 20, 52
comptrollers, 19
continuing education, 45
courses
    college, 23, 24, 27, 35, 39
    high school, 21, 23, 27, 63
cover letters, 28

ABOUT THE AUTHOR

Susan Meyer is a writer living and working in New York City. She has written a number of books for Rosen Publishing. Meyer manages to balance her own checkbook with reasonable success, and, thanks to user-friendly accounting software, has filed her own taxes correctly every year.

PHOTO CREDITS

Cover (figure) © iStockphoto.com/ShutterWorx; cover (background), p. 1 © iStockphoto.com/Tom Abraham; pp. 4, 18–19 Andrey Popov/Shutterstock.com; p. 9 Norman Pogson/ Shutterstock.com; pp. 10–11 Paul Thomas/The Image Bank/ Getty Images; p. 14 BananaStock/Thinkstock; p. 17 Stock4B-RF/Getty Images; p. 20 Fuse/Thinkstock; pp. 22–23, 25, 54–55 © AP Images; pp. 27, 41 iStockphoto/Thinkstock; p. 30 Stockbyte/Thinkstock; pp. 32–33 Stephen Coburn/ Shutterstock.com; p. 36 Robert Kneschke/Shutterstock.com; pp. 38–39 Alexander Raths/Shutterstock.com; pp. 44 Commercial Eye/Iconica/Getty Images; p. 47 Yo Oura/ Photonica/Getty Images; pp. 48–49, 56–57 Pressmaster/ Shutterstock.com; p. 50 JGI/Jamie Grill/Blend Images/Getty Images; pp. 60–61 Justin Sullivan/Getty Images; pp. 62–63 StockLite/Shutterstock.com; back cover (background) © iStockphoto.com/blackred.

Designer: Matt Cauli; Photo Researcher: Karen Huang